SESAME STREET

A DOG'S BEST FRIEND

A Sesame Street Guide to Caring for Your Dog

Marie-Therese Miller

Lerner Publications ◆ Minneapolis

A new dog is an exciting addition to the family, and your friends from *Sesame Street* are here to help you be a responsible pet owner. Learn how to take care of your new pet by helping with things like food, walks, bath time, and cuddles. Along the way you'll learn lifelong lessons about caring for others. With the help of this guide, you and your dog will become furry friends forever, just like Elmo and Tango!

—Sincerely, the Editors at Sesame Street

TABLE OF CONTENTS

 Your New Dog

You got a new dog! Dogs are fun to play with and to cuddle. You have a new friend to love.

You will need to prepare before you bring your dog home. Dogs need:

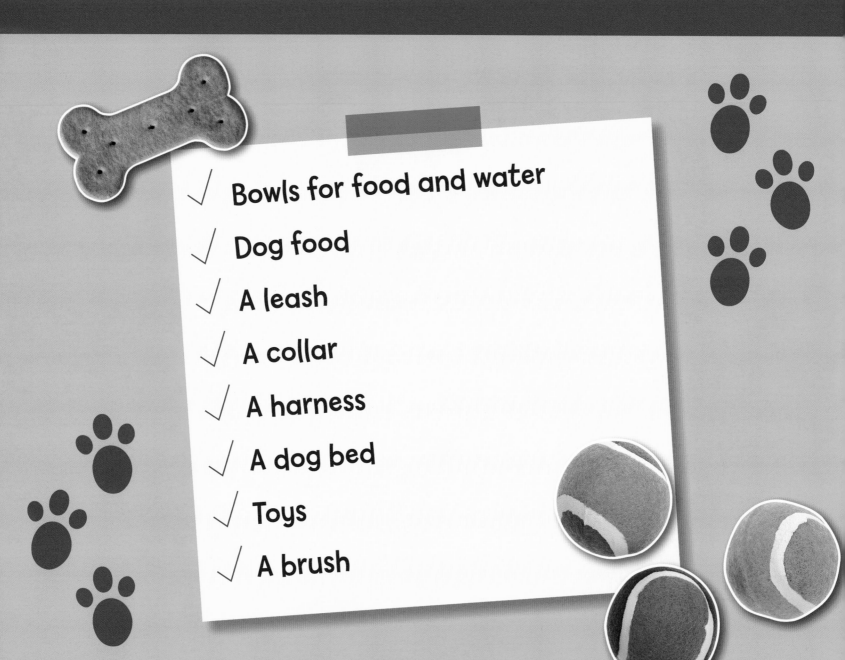

✓ Bowls for food and water

✓ Dog food

✓ A leash

✓ A collar

✓ A harness

✓ A dog bed

✓ Toys

✓ A brush

At first, your dog has to get used to you and their new home. Let the dog come and sniff the back of your hand. Let them explore their new space.

Dogs want their homes to feel "just right."

What will you name your dog? You can give the dog a human name, such as Greyson or Ava. Or you could name them after your favorite food, like Meatball or Muffin.

You have to take care of your dog. For some dog care activities, like going for walks, you will need an adult's help.

You can also pet your dog's fur gently. Sharing time with your dog can make you both happy.

Rose helps Julia feel calm.

Playing is a fun way for dogs to get exercise and stay healthy. Toss a ball for your pup to catch. Run races together outside. Give your furry friend safe toys made just for dogs.

Dogs need food and water every day to stay healthy. Ask an adult to help you. Place dog food in one bowl. Fill another bowl with clean water. You can feed them healthy treats once in a while.

Keep your dog clean. When they are dirty,
an adult can help you give your dog a bath
in warm water. Use special dog shampoo.
Afterward, dry them with a towel. Your dog
may also need their fur brushed regularly.

Dogs need to go outside for bathroom breaks. You and a grown-up can take your dog for walks. Clip a leash to their harness, and off you go! It is good for your dog to meet other people and other pets.

Dogs enjoy hearing kind words. You might say, "Good dog" or "I love you."

In Spanish, we say, "Buen perro" or "Te quiero."

You and a grown-up can teach your dog skills. Dogs can learn to sit, lie down, come, and stay. They can even learn fun tricks, such as shaking hands or rolling over.

It is important to keep your dog healthy. A dog has to go to the veterinarian for regular checkups. You can keep your dog company during the doctor visit.

Dogs need checkups just like we do.

Dogs also need some time alone. For example, let your dog eat without being bothered. Dogs might want to sleep quietly in their own bed.

27

You and your dog will be good friends. You will spend lots of happy times together and love each other for many years.

A dog will be your forever friend!

Help a Shelter Animal

A shelter is a place where animals stay until someone brings them home to love and care for them forever. Here are ways that you and the adults in your life can work together to help a shelter animal:

- Donate old towels and blankets to an animal shelter to help keep the animals warm and comfortable.

- For your next birthday party, ask friends to bring an item that you can give to an animal shelter.

- Some animal shelters let kids read books to the animals. Call to see if your local shelter does this. If not, ask if you can help start a reading program there.

- Organize a donation drive. Decide on a day and place. Get the word out through posters. Ask people to bring items the animal shelter needs.

Glossary

exercise: physical movement done to stay healthy

explore: to look around and discover things

harness: straps that fit around a dog's body and can be attached to a leash

skill: the ability to do something well

sniff: to smell

veterinarian: a doctor who takes care of animals and helps keep them healthy

Learn More

de la Bédoyère, Camilla. *From Puppy to Dog*. Minneapolis: Quarto, 2019.

DK. *The Everything Book of Dogs & Puppies*. New York: DK Children, 2018.

Geister-Jones, Sophie. *Dogs*. Minneapolis: Pop!, 2020.

Index

Photo Acknowledgments

Image credits: Inti St Clair/Getty Images, p. 4; Africa Studio/Shutterstock.com, p. 4 (right); Richard Peterson/Shutterstock.com, p. 6 (brown dog bone); BW Folsom/Shutterstock.com, p. 6 (rubber balls); Ksenia Raykova/Getty Images, p. 7; THEPALMER/E+/Getty Images, p. 8; BG-FOTO/Shutterstock.com, p. 9 (top); monkeybusinessimages/Getty Images, p. 10; TeamDAF/Shutterstock.com, p. 12; FocusStocker/Shutterstock.com (soccer ball), p. 13; damedeeso/iStock/Getty Images, p. 14; Charlotte Amelia Poe/iStock/Getty Images, p. 15; ElenaYakimova/Shutterstock.com, p. 16; Evgeniyqw/Shutterstock.com, p. 17; Teresa Kopec/Moment/Getty Images, p. 18; Javier Brosch/Shutterstock.com, p. 19 (top); Terry Vine/DigitalVision/Getty Images, p. 20; Jose Luis Pelaez Inc/DigitalVision/Getty Images, p. 21 (top); Yuri_Arcurs/E+/Getty Images, p. 22; Jagodka/Shutterstock.com, p. 23 (right); Vesnaandjic/Getty Images, p. 24; GoodLifeStudio/Getty Images, p. 25; cmannphoto/Getty Images, p. 26; gollykim/agency/Getty Images, p. 27 (top); NoSystem images/Getty Images, p. 28; alexei_tm/iStock/Getty Images, p. 29 (top).

Cover: Africa Studio/Shutterstock.com; Richard Peterson/Shutterstock.com; BW Folsom/Shutterstock.com.

To my family, John, Meghan, John Vincent, Erin, Elizabeth, Michelle, and Greyson, thank you for loving me. And to Charbonne and Oreo, thank you for being my dogs.

Lerner Publications Company
An imprint of Lerner Publishing Group, Inc.
241 First Avenue North
Minneapolis, MN 55401 USA

For reading levels and more information, look up this title at www.lernerbooks.com.

Main body text set in Mikado Medium.
Typeface provided by HVD Fonts.

Editor: Andrea Nelson **Designer:** Emily Harris

Library of Congress Cataloging-in-Publication Data

Names: Miller, Marie-Therese, author.
Title: A dog's best friend: a Sesame Street guide to caring for your dog / Marie-Therese Miller.
Description: Minneapolis: Lerner Publications, [2022] | Includes bibliographical references and index. | Audience: Ages 4–8 | Audience: Grades K–1 | Summary: "Celebrate all there is to love about getting a new dog with Sesame Street! Coinciding with the introduction of Tango, Elmo's new puppy, this book will introduce young readers to caring for a new dog"—Provided by publisher.
Identifiers: LCCN 2020050267 (print) | LCCN 2020050268 (ebook) | ISBN 9781728424255 (library binding) | ISBN 9781728431406 (paperback) | ISBN 9781728430447 (ebook)
Subjects: LCSH: Dogs—Juvenile literature.
Classification: LCC SF427 .M584 2022 (print) | LCC SF427 (ebook) | DDC 636.7/083—dc23

LC record available at https://lccn.loc.gov/2020050267
LC ebook record available at https://lccn.loc.gov/2020050268

Manufactured in the United States of America
1-49295-49411-5/7/2021